The Melody Of Emotion

Daniel Montez Barnes

Published by Daniel Montez Barnes, 2019.

The melody
of
emotions

Poetry that Express changing with the changing of time

By: Daniel Barnes

Introduction

The description of poetry can only be felt by emotions which theoretically emotions can be affected by season. The melody of emotions is just that, a changing with the changing of time. Just like emotions does on a regular to every individuals. From the four season recongnized

and labeled to the Main emotions of love and more. Comes a intriguing read that will make you drawn to share as well as utilized in everyway.

A book of poetry upholding the define spoken word and the root of true rhythm with meaning and vivid illustration. So open yourself to the metaphor and poetic trance that will definitely grab and take you within the melodies of emotions.

Enjoy.

THE MELODY OF EMOTION

First edition. June 19, 2019.

Copyright © 2019 Daniel Montez Barnes.

ISBN: 978-1735599014

Written by Daniel Montez Barnes.

Table of Contents

Chapter 1
March 1ˢᵗ – May 31st

The love that one another share as the calming breeze brings the environment to a sense of peace. Joy and care with thought. Only can the season of spring bring forth giving and creation which is categorized as number one and the beginning of change.

Complete

You feel me up and make me whole more than you can think of, from head to toe you touch my soul filling my heart with love. You can take a piece of the pie but it's like it never been gone, as I look deep into your eyes it's like I'm already home.

I think of you all the time because you're my other half, you're always on my mind like the leg to a crab, just to see your face would mean the whole world to me, with looks I love to taste that makes up our recipe.

Now that I'm so far away I feel like I am torn apart, I take it easy day by day as you're the light to my dark . you make me what I am completing me as a man, and just like a dam you hold water for the land.

With you as my girl on any task and you are the pearls behind all my exotic mask. I see that you're there even in this situation, when family don't even dare being evolved during the duration. that's why I say you like the flower and I'm like the stem, together we hold the power connected like a limb.

I wish you knew how deep I truly feel, because I speak the facts to what is even more real. This is a bond between me and you, we make up a team that's equal up to two, Maybe its just us but like the Navy we are like a fleet, being with you is a must cause you make me complete.

My girls Valentines

I'm writing you these few lines to the girl I consider mind, sweeter than candy with a heart that's kind. I think about you all the time with radiant skin and eyes like wine. I had to let you know what's on my mind, for now at the end of this rhyme I just wanted to say Happy Valentine's.

Breathtaking

Every time I look at you my breath you take away, and then I glanced at your physic that's smoother than Santa's sleigh. As I tried to inhale it seems as though I cannot breathe, but when I feel your touch it seems to put me right at ease. Sometimes my stomach feel as though its full of thin air and as I talk to you I hope that you're not aware. Then I think to myself what's in the making, to start I had to let you know it's pleasant that you are breathtaking.

Four letters

To show compassion or show that I care, to give you my heart without any fear. To tell you my deepest darkest secret but to another I rather keep it. To give you my warmth when you're cold from my body I will, to be your guard, sword, and shield to protect you is how I truly feel. I summarized it down to four simple letters, something that's strong but light as a feather. Love is the only word, not a noun or a verb something inside that I always show, and from the heart is shall always grow.

My heart

My heart pounds at the thought of you, everything you say is Right on cue. Your the only woman that can do the things you do to get through to me.

Your looks are sharper than a pair of cutters is always makes my heart beat flutter, and you seem to know what to utter that can make a blind man see.

When it comes down to my heart no one can never tear us apart, they can be sweet sour or tart but you're the one that holds the key.

Delicate Flower

Your like a Bud that blossoms into a beautiful flower with a structure that's right for the picking. The stem that holds its own shape, a figure which is so elegant, rugged but smooth being tender underneath. Appealing like a Rose, Daisy or dandelion. A plant that bears the seeds uprooted by photosynthesis, me being the source of energy in carbohydrates to synthesize your innermost form. The leaf which makes up your individuality, single in kind with its own excellence and design. Fine in the petals which has its own independency. Strong enough to endure any type of weather that has a tendency to be vulnerable to a manly touch. **You are my delicate flower.**

Your exceptional

Your exceptional just by your personality, and ever since we met You have Been my reality.

Your exceptional by the way you care, in every moment you was always there.

Your exceptional because how you understand, and whatever that I came up with your always with the plan.

Your exceptional because you do what you say and every time I Had a idea you made it appear in a way.

Your exceptional on how you know what's on my mind every time we have a problem you seem to get us out of the bind.

Three Dimensional when it comes to me your like a professional, and when it comes to everything your exceptional.

Memories

I remember the first thought when I seen you and ask myself could it be true. I knew then I had to have you in my life if not as my woman that's my wife. The vibe was there straight from the start, and the openness that we share automatically stole my heart. From the good through the bad you have always been there, even through the times I thought nobody cared. what's mine is yours and what's yours is mine, and to be with you in my life there's not enough time. A wise woman once said I need another hour and a day, to express how I truly feel through the words I say. Until death do us part I'll embrace your loving energy, as we create more of these cherishable sweet memories.

Love you more than words

I love you more than words can describe, but what I can say with you is how I want to strive.

How I feel about you is hard to write on paper, because the love is so deep, it'll be something you want to savor.

The love I have for you is more abundant than the earth, even so valuable that it's priceless with significant worth.

To tell you the truth you really drive me crazy, having me think about a ring attached to a lovely lady.

The love I have for you is more than child's play, but I'll leave it at that because I love you more than words can say.

In my heart

In my heart is where I hold you close, and that's where I keep things that matters the most. To the rhythm you add to my beat, that seems to lift me off my feet.

But truly you're the one that keeps me going, and also get my blood to flowing.

Even when I lay down to bed, not only are you in my heart but you're in my head.

I don't think my heart would ever stop,
but without you my heart May pop.

In my heart you shall forever be, until the last but never least end of me.

Penetration of my heart

You cut my heart open like a slicer to a cake, and you couldn't even sell it back up if I had stitches along with tape.

You slice me quickly like a razor to the skin, and I bleed profusely even though you say you won't do it again.

You chop my heart in half like I'm the tree and you're the a, but I still love you like music turned up to the max.

You peel me wide open like a knife cutting butter, and the wound is so deep that I barely know the words to utter.

You make an incision on my heart that's beneath the surface, but I know the things you do always serve a general purpose.

You make a gash through my heart like a chainsaw to a block of wood, and something keep telling me that you have to be some good.

you scratch my heart that opens me up inside and even though you hurt me, to you I still with loyalty abide.

I grabbed the blade even though I know that it's sharp, but I think I'm just addicted to your penetration of my heart.

Comparing candy to your love

Your love is like a box of chocolate candy or a pixie stick tasting sweet but yet Sandy, and you will always be my curse as your lips are juicier than a red "starburst".

Your Love answer all my wishes, and is more tasteful then a pack of "Hershey kisses". You being that delightful treat, something I would like to devour and eat.

Your body being something I would have for lunch, and more tastier than a "Nestle crunch"

Your love is something that will never linger, and always will stay with me like a "Butterfinger"

Sounding more lovelier than a soft playing fiddle, and is sweeter than a big bag of "Skittles".

Your love is all the special cravings, with no expiration that is really more worth saving.

Intimacy

Intimacy comes from the heart of the soul, something more valuable than money or gold. intimacy is something you just jump up and do without your lover ever having a clue.

like bringing a lit candle to the kitchen table, then turning the lights down as if you're in a fable.

Intimacy is showing how romantic you are, no matter how close and definitely no matter how far. Intimacy gives off so much emotion, and makes your spouse feel as if they're floating.

Intimacy can pick you up when you're feeling down **intimacy** can make your whole relationship go round.

Unspeakable emotion

This unspeakable emotion I can't even describe, it's hard to even tell when you look upon my eyes. When I tried to tell you it's hard to come out my mouth, because it's stuck in my heart deep down in the South.

Even though when I'm with you, you fill me with so much joy, like a little kid playing with a untypical toy. When I tell you this it would be hard to explain, but if I keep it bottled up it would be hard round you to maintain.

That's why I'm writing you here, now, today. so I can tell you how I feel in every unspeakable way. I love you so much from the bottom of my soul you and me would be something I would truly like to mold. when you're with me you will never be afraid, cause when I'm with you I feel like I have every battle made.

Us being together will flow like the ocean, all this I have written is to you, from my unspeakable emotion.

The truth

I want to take the time to apologize, that I came to my sense to realize what I have in front of my eyes.

I'm sorry for the things I took you through, I'm sorry for the things that I know I do. I'm sorry for the bad and hard times, I'm saying I'm sorry while I read these lines.

You stick with me through thick and thin, I say to myself this can't happen again. I know I might have done the same old thing, I'm taking this time to think and change.

We're stronger together like a flock of birds, my actions will speak louder than these words. I know you do what you have to do, so you can look out for me and you. Next time when round your neck you feel that noose, remember I'm sorry and that's the truth.

<u>Together</u>

We stick together like two feathers or a two-piece suit made out of leather.

We stick together like white on rice, or two pair of shoes. You being the left with me as your right.

we stick together like husband and wife, or better yet like butter to bread with a knife.

we stick together like creatures in the ocean, or getting sea sickness because of the our emotions.

we stick together like tile on the floor, or like hinges are attached to a invincible door. Together forever will forever be together forever you and me.

<u>Love</u>

Love is a powerful saying, love is more than words by man.

love it can be a tricky thing,

love can be all it means.

love can be that you care so much,

love can be to feel that person's touch.

love can be like a bag of chips,

love could be like the cream and dip.

love could be so believably true, love can be with me and you.

Chapter 2

June 1st – August 31st

Summer a delightful light which has it's toil on nature but also the mind of man & individuals alike. A fact to be harmful in many ways than one. This unveils the dreadfulness of life and the struggles that seem dark in the brightest of time. A road from what seem like peace to a light that is overbearing if utilized in a different way. Knowing what you may see in beauty around you only to cause famine pushing mother nature and most into dismay.

The summer shine

A gleam that comes from the sky with dude I'm revealing the blemishes the melody mix with heat as a street gives off vapor from the moist concrete the constant pain duration of the rain in the body except which we supply fluids to maintain and sustain life and what it contains a steady cycle which comes around out of one of the two that can be unbearable so and water we drown with a screen to enjoy this light to prevent outcome of this terrible but the enjoyment just to be within is one is like being a secret admirer and finally getting close to who you desire the radiant energy that it holds to generate mechanisms synergy illuminate our surroundings as it enhances our perceptions in vibrant colors as it also serves as a light to our direction in completing the task ahead the summer shine revolves around the Central Star takes his place on a specific time which is statistically met beginning with a glorious up rise ending with a beautiful sunset.

Persuasive

There's a lot of smooth talkers in this world that runs a lot of game but if you ever listen to them is pretty much all the same their main objective is getting what they came for out of you not if you listen long enough they'll get you to they come in our age and sizes from big to small and it will be a little kid guaranteed to get it all also watch out for the ones that talk very fast because they're the ones that only look for bits of quick cash before you know it they're going without louvers passivation so watch out for them folks that I call persuasive.

The jungle

The world is just like a jungle filled with insects and beast different species together in a bundle North South West and East. Some people are like bees buzzing around your head some people are like monkeys listen to what he and she said then there are the strong that prey on the weak even though the wrong there after what they see now and every jungle there's a king that tries to control everything you might hear sounds of voices that sing, but even in the jungle everything is not what it seems.

Changing Seasons

As the world turns we have changing seasons, which affect how we act, what we wear and other suitable reasons. It all depends on where you are for that time of year, because when you think it's going to rain it can be sunny and clear.

Usually around January it be nice and cold, **winter** takes no prisoners knowing you'll outside froze.

Then up comes the **summer** when it's scorching hot and in the month of July we show off, visiting those favorite spots.

After that the Leo month "August" creeps in, and its the **spring** where the leaves in the trees start to blend.

Fall pops up unannounced and leaving us with a mess, October we clean up our yard as we prepare our nest.

Now it's like a revolving door because the winter just committed treason, but it's how we exist because of these relevant changing seasons. "**Food for thought**"

How we look

How we look usually affects the way we act, changing our attitude because of what we have on our back. Not only what we wear but how we look in the face, seeing something we dislike rather than accept it we have it replaced.

If we enjoy what we typically have on, it contribute to our moral values and set a certain tone. what matters the most is our outer appearance, people look at it first that should aid us to sustain perseverance. It gives us comfort in articulate areas, so when you're nervous were able to break down barriers.

We are observed by what we wear, individuals are judgmental so its always good to care. Some people feel as if they don't look good, but dress to impress for yourself just to know that you could.

we might not be seen as models or characters in a book, but I call it unique by the difference of how we look.

Short days and long nights

I go to sleep to hear my doors locked, and wake up to hear my doors pop. To think that it is all in my head, I put on my slippers as I hop out of bed.

We hang out for about an hour, things being in Balance because of money and the power. as I lay on the yard looking up at the sun, my eyes shine brightly as the clouds run.

And so the day ends I find myself in a bunk, I toss and turn of the thoughts oh how deep I have sunk.

Two hours or more after they turn off the lights, I lay awake wondering about the short days and these long nights.

Poor life

from jelly and no bread to grits and no eggs this is what you call poor. When the milk man can't even sit a glass of milk by your door.

As you go to work doing a nine-to-five it still feels like you're taking a big nose dive. While you struggle to make all your ends meet, you take a deep breath and portray a façade of no defeat. knowing that today you have did what you can, you try to devise yet another plan. other people look at you as if you know not left from right. Just show them what the best is in a classified poor life.

Pain

From the suffering to the Shane, from The hunger to the pain. These are the things we take on our journey, to the trials and tribulation we make for our attorney. As the pain we endure, this in our heart we try to stay pure. from the dark we look around to see people hurt and cry, while the homeless lay in the dark we wonder why. we think to our self did we make these decisions or is it for our health that we see these visions. In our walk through the seasons I hear the talk that certain pain happens for a reason.

Laugh now cry later

We laugh now and cry later so we can be that participator. in these activities, in these game so we don't have to feel ashamed. some people say things that they don't mean, we try to laugh it off and work as a team. to walk off like we don't care, but in the inside we are full of tears. we try to keep a persona of Joy, so they don't see The real "McCoy". but when

people want to be a hater, laugh now cry later.

The past

A person once told me don't dwell on the past, when it comes it goes and you're done with that task. whatever it was is gone for a fact, you moved on with your future never to look back. everybody makes mistakes, you live and you learn from what it takes. some things in your past you want to change, but in all reality it remains the same. All you can do is correct it now and never let the past get you down.

Regret

People are full of a lot of regret, for the things they've done in the past and people they neglect. feeling sorry for the things they do, wanted to go back and start a new. while you go on to make things right, other people rather reframe from your sight. so when you feel down don't you fret because those other people also have regret.

Wrong and right

Where's there's right then comes wrong, when things get tight people change their tone. it's easy to do wrong then it is to do right, it's stick to you like a prick that you're trying to fight. it's a mix of Good and evil like choosing to have chicken pox or the measles. As you pick between right and wrong, think about your life and your own. Doing wrong might seem right, as you make a decision don't lose sight.

Nobody knows

Nobody knows what a person go through, nobody knows what a person really do. Nobody knows what a person is secretly tell, nobody knows when a person is going through hell.

Nobody knows how a person lives his life, nobody knows that that person carries a knife Nobody knows how that person feel inside, nobody knows where that person have to hide. when it comes to Nobody knows, it give you a chance to stay on your toes. but there's one person that always see, and that's the power above you and me.

Games we play

The games we played could go either way, it could bring someone to you or leave them astray. some games are good to relieve the stress, some games we play put you to the test. Games we play could make you insane, it could be mental like being high in a plane, it could be physical to the touch, the games we play we could love so much. The games we play could be financial, like taking money out of someone's mantle. The games we play to make us happy or sad, the games we played to be good or bad.

The king of the jungle

The king of the jungle is the greatest monster, even his roar sounds like thunder. eating everything in his sight, crushing the bones with all his might. The king run the lands here and yonder, never taken the time to sit and wonder. running fast like you never seen before, poucing on his victims from the back door. Known a the king and in the jungle the main, where he is on the top of our list an number one in the food chain.

The Earth

The Earth is such a beautiful place. A beautiful race now today we make mistakes polluting the land and even the lakes people act like they don't even care selling the land that's not even theirs cutting the trees down by the pears to the animals is just not fair this is to our generation try to provide for our nation just for what is truly worth do your best to protect this sacred Earth.

The rain

The rain it comes the rain that goes when will it stop nobody knows. sometimes it rain hard sometimes it drizzled when it hits the ground sometimes sizzles. when it snow sometimes it rain, it also comes with hurricanes. it to feel like you're not getting wet at all then get drenched as you walk in the mall. just like my sister use to say rain, rain go away. **"Food for thought"**

Temptation

Temptation is a tricky game, it can lead you back to the same thing. when you try to avoid what you can't quit, it comes back hard just to stick. it's like trying to stop a habit, running around trying to catch that rabbit. Temptation can be good or it can be bad, it can drive a person insane or mad. so to temptation this is what I say, try to utilize it in a positive type of way.

We talk but nobody listen

We open our mouths so we can be heard. We want people to listen to every single word. even when we speak on all the facts, they close their ears and turn their back. It can be the people that's so close, the ones that we really love the most. from your cousin, your auntie, your sister, or brother, to your uncle , your niece and nephew or mother. it can't be too short it can't be too long, cause when we talk we're always wrong. even when we say something we know they heard, the truth they always come back with something else absurd, it always seems like something is missin because when we talk nobody listen.

Gimmie

Gimmie is when you really want that, but Gimmie will make that person hold it back. gimmie is the person that's so impatient, Gimmie will always keep that person waiting. every time Gimmie have something to say, just so Gimmie can have it his or her way. Gimmie always have a corny excuse, so that Gimmie gets what it wants and turn us loose. Gimmie is the close to all your open doors, Gimmie is a word not called for. Gimmie always catches us at home, Gimmie knows when we're at the house alone. but when Gimmie ever come to my spot, I always tell them that Gimmie got shot.

The hidden passage

S kip the formalities cost in one we are all the same, but I'm here to speak on principalities and in life how we must sustain.

I could talk about Scrappy or how Miami won another ring this year, but why when we failed to open our eyes to see individual still living in fear.

I could blame the system and say why didn't they make that change, but we don't use our own mind knowing together things can be rearranged.

Now don't get me wrong the world itself its a dirty place, but we must have patients even if the time seemed long remembering the turtle won the race.

Somebody once said the early bird gets the worm, but I know the first to be last and the last to be first. plus with life you live and you learn, and with the gathering of knowledge you'll never thirst.

We must seek truth because there's always more than what life tell us, while righteously Guiding your heart avoiding envy, jealousy and lust.

Among temptation we attack one another in obtaining things for our own sake, in the end we'll see who calls who brother but when that happens it will be far too late.

In all what I'm trying to say it's the route along with the decisions we make, a wise woman once said you have to pay to play and what you get you received by what you allow yourself to take.

N ow this is the conclusion: "you are who you say you are rather below or above the average, but I have observed resolution and it's all within this hidden passage".

Chapter 3
September 1st – November 30th

The third statistically is fall, in hindsight is the acceptance and contentment of what has come to be after the destruction and/or production in what has passed. The journey of knowing upon actions and experiences. Striving to advance in what we know, to have unexpectancy and regulations within the land. As the cycle continues to reap what you have sowed, sort of speak from season before. With more to offer, But even tornadoes can this time of year... Food for thought

Commitment

A bond between two people, a pledge or promise to what you put your heart into. taking responsibility which derived from Love, instilled in discipline having self-control while upholding your vows, being faithful upon dedication to the goals you have set out to achieve. what you're trying to obtain self-approval, respect, or a firm relationship summarize as commitment. stepping up to the plate not only to serve but to participate in the feast to success. staying grounded is the key to the result you long for, but have to attempt to partake in the game before you can win the prize.

The families Turkey

Every Thanksgiving giving my uncle tried to catch it, and he make sure it's the fattest one he gets. afterwards he gives it to Grandma to begin the job, as my cousin prepare the right greens and corn on the cob. Grandma grab it by the neck and cut off the head, to my surprise he still runs around after I thought it was already dead. then she passed it to auntie that pluck off the feathers and there are so many you can feel up a pillow made of leather. they passed it to me and I passed it to my brother, they told him to take out the guts he passed it to another. when I see the outcome I rather eat beef jerky, but who am I kidding I'm about to enjoy this families Turkey.

Motion of life

You sway back and forth trying to catch your grip, every time you try to stand you always seem to slip. you proceeded to move forward suddenly you hit a wall, but when it's time to move on, you learn how to catch your fall. even as you grow it feels like you haven't moved, but like a wise person once told me what you don't use you'll lose.

From what I know

From what I know I learned from the best, and the rest I know comes from my common sense. now this is what I learned from the wise, close my mouth and opening my eyes. everything that glitters may not be gold, and everything that appears new might just be old. what we do to a person reflect upon the next man, which might prevent them from extracting a new plan.

Each day you make up for what you didn't in the past, and prepare for tomorrow as if it's your last. follow the spirit and never the flesh, obey the laws to stay up the mess.

This is from what I know, to the highest of the highs and the lowest of the low. now this is what I know from just being me, a kind of fact ordinary people can't see. from what I know the skies is black people say is blue because at the time it's that. Take away the sun, moon, and the stars, and the only blue you'll see is from the headlight of your cars.

from what I know where made from Sand, and not from monkey made up by man. just look at the way that we are created, so unique that only God could have made it.

From what I know I can knock down any wall, without any breaks or no stalls. It can be metal wood or even brick, I will not it down bit by bit. I step up to it just like a door, and knock down it to the floor. I never said it would hit the ground all I spoke on is knocking it down. now this is from what I know, common sense and that's for show.

Christmas joy

Today is the day of happiness and cheer, and even if it rained you can still see clear. when all your problems seem to disappear as the drink is jugs of soy.

A day where a child was born, with a heart that can never be torn. to the word he was sworn, which is the birth of a brand new boy.

Our thoughts may be on family we love the most, or wish that with others we could be close. but for them we hold a toast, giving to the unfortunate that can't receive that toy.

We set out this day to have a feast, to help others that have the least. we seek out this day of peace, while we filled with Christmas joy.

Bring me home

There's a place I rather be that's glorious to go, with no lock doors and a river of milk that flow. The sun is so bright that you can barely look at it, where people State truth and not man-made facts. Jewels that special with a precious glaze, in a huge kingdom that's probably something like a maze. This is something that you only dream about, or only hear with your ears by words of my mouth. it's a place that consist of lovely Roses and beautiful flowers, with no concerns of money, respect, or power. that's why I have no worries about me being gone, because when it's all said and done I know that I'll be right at home.

Five fingers

For every finger on one hand they all serve a purpose, some mean more than others and others that use is surplus. for starters, the thumb is a sign of a good job working and mean okay, you can even signal a ride if you're in a little delay.

A index finger is used to point a person in the right direction, it can wag left and right saying no at a person's discretion.

the middle finger means one thing and that is forget you, and if you don't know what it stands for all I can say is get a clue.

A ring finger is exactly just what it stands for, such as love, friendship, or a diamond when you take a step through that door.

The pinky finger can mean many things, the classy people extended it to let you know they're higher than the average bean. some people wear rings giving off the impression of a pimp, but in their pockets they're really broke that's why they have a walk with that limp.

Every ligament express your demeanor so pay close attention to how you use your five fingers.

My uniform

There is all types of uniforms that means one particular things, but my uniform itself gives off all kinds of means. The uniform can tell you what I've been through, all you have to do is look and I can show you. it also tells you that I'm a real man, because behind the uniform these guys are not what they're portraying. my uniform can also tell you when I'm ready for battle, maybe not on land but my horse I can saddle. one day to you my uniform I'll send, but just to let you know my uniform is me in my skin.

Your creation

The sites that we see are so exhilarating, and the sound behind them are even more fascinating. the Earth you made was once just a circle, before the colors of green, yellow, and purple. then he said let there be light, which was the sun that shines so bright. after that he added the stars and the moon, to uplift the night I would assume. Along with the sky they all combined, which change with the changing of the season in time. he created the land, and all he did was speak the words and so it began. from the cows, the fish, and even the pigs. to the grass, flowers, even the little twigs. All which I can say was in good health, even the man that was made with a single breath. now all around it diplomatic with different plantations, but nobody would even exist if it wasn't for your creation.

E thnic group
    Black, Puerto Rican, Dominican, and Asian, even down to the white Caucasian. we was once one whole nation, but I infatuation led to our separation.

Now we're all scattered amongst the land, with different cultures being our own man. as people now have a different talk, that goes along with their certain walk.

Because of our ethnic traits people take advantage, somehow we always seem to adapt with what's managed. Others not realizing we once was all brothers, that helped out, aided, and took care of one another.

They'll come a time forced are we joined together, through the light and Stormiest of weather. just like when the birds in the sky form that loop. We will once again be one whole ethnic group. "**Food for thought**"

A round the world

around the world there's different things, different meanings, people with different dreams. we can sit down and let the world turn, or venture out and experience in that we should learn. Around the world it's a amazing sight, stuff you can enjoy with the average life. from exotic food to the casual wear. From the luxury bars that's along with the creepy pair. Even down to the money that we spend, some big bills and some real thin. As we step into another atmosphere, we see new things and swallow our fears. people giving us that unusual look, some welcoming and some who are shook. but treat this life as if it was your pearl, pack your bags and travel around "within" the world.

To grow

To perceive in life just to grow, we learned a lot about the show. we ask questions just to know, so we can stay constant on the go. just like a stream or a steady flow, or standing up on your own with one toe. even if you're okay or poor, you keep on going to learn some more. just to avoid that foe, you stay high so you don't go low. That day come before you say the word so, with that in this life you have to grow.

Manage

In this life you have to manage, knowing that it comes with a disadvantage. trying to maintain a stable household, feeling as if you have no control. while you work to hold a job, it still feels like you've been robbed. to make money just to pay these bills, now empty-handed you feel ill. to manage these things is no fun, for your happy to see now that they're done.

Now and later

People live for now rather than living for later, instead of buying food they buy a expensive pair of gators. looking at what's in front and not looking ahead, doing things differently than what we initially said. people say tomorrow is not guaranteed, so they buy what they want and not what they need. I say if you want to really live greater, don't think about now but think about later.

The mind

A person wants told me a mind is a terrible thing to waste ,if you don't use it then that could turn into useless paste. knowing stuff that give you knowledge, information that could take you beyond college. you could sit and let your mind seem dead, or you can get up move around and stay ahead. when it comes to a living mind, don't procrastinate or waste any time.

"food for thought"

Human race

When it comes to black, white, or even yellow, no matter if you're a woman or a wonderful fellow. even if you're rich or poor, or a Asian that was knocking at your door. talking with a accent we don't understand, from doing different things in your own land. as we walk a still, steady, speedy Pace, one thing in all is common is that were the human race.

Levels

In life there are a lot of levels, some of us even have several. as we always try to go up, some of us runs out of luck. just to hop up to try it again, never to lose always to win. just to take a little step, every inch always help. when we really come to truly see, is when we where we want to be.

Stories I heard

I heard so many stories in the world, the one about boys and the one about girls. from the story about the birds and the bees, to when man ate from The forbidden tree. From when Humpty Dumpty fell off the wall, to David who made Goliath and more fall. from when Jack and Jill went up the hill, to when the itsy bitsy spider tried to make his first kill. all these stories came from old words, all these stories is from what I heard.

Determination

When it comes to determination, it can lead to your salvation. providing laws for a nation, as Einstein made his quotation, about the world and its rotation. we have to have patience about our infatuation, as everything comes about by our own determination.

Reverse

Sometimes we go in full reverse, going after things to satisfy our thirst. as we get off our course we back tracked. Justifying our source reframing from the fact. just like a train hopping off the track, or like a dog trying to find his way back. for example for a pair of shoes, we do things that we used to do. or just for that certain way of life, we do things that we know are not right. so just to avoid all of this which is a simple curse, forward is the drive so you will not get stuck in reverse.

Natural high

As the Cool breeze touch my face, the clean air I give a taste. I breathe in and out a sigh of relief, now it is to my knowingly belief, the naturalness of a high, without that given substance but looking at the sky. I wonder and ponder to the sensation, a natural high now my mental and physical fluctuation.

Me myself and I

Me, myself, and I, that's what most people say, thinking only about themselves in a selfish kind of way. while they walk by seeing people in need, and they wonder why we have a messed up community. at the end of the day when it's all said and done, think about me myself and I is really a battle inside that's never won.

Mother's day

On this day I give you thanks, as you birth me into this world of ranks. you held me, fed me, and clothed me good. everything you taught me I understood. you made me happy with what we had, even when I made you mad. we always made up again and again, even through the thick and thin. Now, today and ahead, I love you so and wanted to say, have a wonderful mother's day.

People say

People say this and that, stuff which is not even a fact, thinking that they know what's up, to keep on talking and it's never enough. instead of listening to what they heard, they like to listen to their own words. now some things people say are true, it relates to me and relates to you. they've been where you have to go, they know what you have yet to know. so when you hear people say, those words use in your own way.

My mama told me

My mama told me to keep your head up because you never know when somebody wants to be tough.

My mama told me don't let them ride your bike, because some of these kids are just not right.

My mama told me never to do wrong, because your days will be short rather than long.

My mama told me to always stay true, and do unto others as you have them do unto you.

My mama told me to do what's right, because the truth will come eventually to the light.

My mama told me to stand up on your own, because you never know when you'll be all alone.

My mama told me watch The company you keep, because they will get you while your asleep.

My mama told me not to trust what don't grow. my mama told me all this because she know.

Up and down

What goes up must come down, gravitation won't let it hang around. what goes up might not be rough, but when it comes down it's always tough. just like when you jump in the air, you come back down quicker than a tear. so when you're stuck up with a frown, just know eventually you'll come back down.

Back and forth

We make up each and everyday, go about things different but in the same way. as we trying to make something new, the old is the only thing that we pursue. only to try to make it seem better, it will never change just like the weather. no matter if it's sunny, snow, or rain. what it does will stay the same. you could go east, south, west or north, but in the end you'll still be going back and forth.

My brother

To my brother from you to me, rather by blood or in the street. we keep our word, we keep our bond, no matter if the weight weighs a ton. even though we may argue we keep it tight, making sure things get back right. you had my back through thick and thin, even when I really didn't know you then. even in the stormy weather, we always hung and stuck together. there's never been ever a lie, me and you, we ride or die.

All-for-one one-for-all

All for one and one for all, together we stand divided we fall. as we march to fight for what's right, we cross the lands just to unite. we waited and have all tried to be patient, now we battle for our nation. rather its physical or mental gain, long as we believe and make a change. Because nothing ever stays the same, long as you have more than just a brain. you have to open your mouth to speak, if you want what you see. sometimes you have to use some Force, if you don't have no other choice. it might be best to sit and wonder, instead of being trapped in the thunder. long as it's for your loved ones, everything is said and already done. your back against the corner of the wall, it's all for one and one for all. **"Food for thought"**

Time and time Again

Time and time again it seems like the same thing, in a different way we do the same routine.

We wake up to the same old dream, to hang out with the same old team.

On another path to the same scene, in a circle as it's to a ring.

Connected together like birds with wings, flying around as it hums and sings.

But even birds can get off balance as its sore and leans, just like a bad habit is to a fiend. Time and time again is the crop of the cream, but time and time again is not always what it means.

What we do

What we do always reflect upon us, even those we love, rely on, and trust.

from looking at people with full of doubt, to the way we talk, scream, and shout.

we should always treat people like we want to be treated, not thinking that we are overly exceeded.

We can also be extremely uptight, and feel like we're doing the things that's right.

As we buy the things we really want, while others have desire for the things they don't.

It can be me or it can be you, let's just watch what we say even more what we do.

Window pane

Looking out my window pane, hopefully it does not rain. my window above me just so bright, and the pane you shine oh so white. on my window pane there is no Mark, only thing I see is the Streaks that's sharp. making sure there is no stains, using polish to Wipe the pane. as a bird leaves it droplets, now I'm ashamed, because I'm never done on the cleaning of my window pane. "**Food for thought**"

Life consistency

We breathe and exist by what comes from nature itself, but then we can terminate the world with the waist that's detrimental to our own health.....

Leading deficiency.

Twisted facts which society Lacks, constructed to distract, what we really feel. contrary to the truth that's real, laws that sealed, but change amongst a deal .....

Considered efficiency.

The mind being built for survival and evolution, now clouded by pollution, which is made from our own hand. but ignoring the cause, like a structure with no walls. we quickly fall into the already predestined quicksand.

Desire persistency.

A battle to sustain, while we maintain, in a civilization that pertains, to what is thought to be right. we must rid the infatuation, and come to a realization, if our Nation, ever want to see the light. or this will be nothing more than ....

Life consistency.

Sensible man and the simpleton

A sensible man thinks before he acts, a simpleton goes into the water not knowing the facts.

A sensible man with issues knows how to solve them, a simpleton create many more problems

A sensible man study and plan, a simpleton jumps in head-first not knowing when.

A sensible man keeps his eyes on the prize, a simpleton man only understand lies.

A sensible man will always remain on top, while the simpleton man will always get stopped. **"Food for thought"**

Right by my side

Out of everything I do I know you're by my side, as long as I stay straight from my face you'll never hide. every time I fall you always do pick me up, it may not be on my time but I know it's not by luck.

when life is getting hard and I don't know what to do, you always show me the way with my hand you lead me through. sometime when I think it's enough and you're done, you bless me even more providing me with a ton.

I know you have a plan and its for me to take. as long as I believe in you myself you will never forsake. even at times when I make mistakes and backslide, I know a higher power is always there right by my side.

The eye opener

Hi ,what's up, greetings, what's happening, what it do? amongst these initiations That's when judgement begins.

When it's all said and done the conversations never through even though every beginning has an end.

Now you don't have to listen to what I have to say, but really I care enough to say it.

This might not be about zone 6, Savannah, or the **A**, but like artist "50 cent" said "give me your attention just a little bit".

Truth be told we walk around blind, most of all we ignore the bigger picture.

being blocked by the decisions of our mind, like the rich who want to become more Richer.

We fail to observe what's right in front of us, when they put enlightenment on every thing that posses a station.

But with each other we rather fight and fuss, not realizing the whole world was once one nation.

Then what get me people say they're real and solid as a brick, but do everything contrary to the truth.

who am I to say because they used to call me slick, but as man it's best to positively inspire the youth.

We can continue to do what we do in these darkest hours, and witness what might unfold.

or we can make a change with all our power, so at least our kids can watch their kids get old.

Jealousy and envy won't get us nowhere, but eventually result into a mutiny.

Just like the disciples without love is not a pair, and light Queen Latifah said we must have U-N-I-T-Y that's unity.

Chapter 4

December 1st – February 28th

A Surprise and anticipation of the end towards a new beginning of what we think is to come. A winter effect that can operate on various levels that leave what has come to be non-existent. We have only what is given as shown to our "eye', and instilled in our "mind'. Winter which is fourth and foremost the most crucial of seasons itself because to have the ability to freeze over symbolically and statistically means that preservation lies in the future to continue. Where the first will be last and the last will be first... food for thought.

<u>Premonition</u>

Have you ever been doing a task that seems as if you did it before, it's like wearing that mask and going through the same door.

you see what happens next but it's only a quick look, sometimes it has you perplexed, or might even have you shook.

this can reveal itself in your dreams, but when you are awake, you can take it for what it change with the choices you make

.

they say it's a blessing and a curse for you to see the future ahead, but nobody coerced us to make the decision that comes after the present which is lead.

this is what I call a God-given gift, or what some people call it a mental condition, to what's Destine it causes a rift, long as you know how to alter your premonition.

Behind closed Doors

Behind closed doors you would never know the truth, it could deal with the mature or even in the youth. we all have secrets that we want to hide, so we keep them behind closed doors rather than outside. it can be small and it can be major, but we keep them locked in a box just like military razors. to reveal these things could be bad for your health, it can even involve serious injury to life and death. for these doors you would need a significant key, and you cannot tell what the eyes may see. some of these tickets have different floors but some things are left better unsaid and even more behind closed doors.

Clear skies

To define my emotions as a man I look up to see the sun shining bright. Anointed, I can feel your presence like the clouds above my head, appellant and gentle.

just like you are
that star, that twinkles in the day and glow at night
just like, a smooth flight, above the land. you make me feel as though I can do more than what I think I can.
its like I can see the other side where me and you reside, transparent like a crystal that just been wiped clean, beautiful on the scene, something like a dream, that just came true.
nothing can blind me from what I observed not even a Scattered shower, or the darkest hour, because together we have the power, to turn on the light.
friendly I realize
that I have closed my eyes

only to open them to still see clear skies.

The one who loves

He is so kind and even more merciful, he knows all and never take things personal. he's the one who walked with us side-by-side, but truly within is where he resides. he carry us when we fall, he always answer when we call. He give us wisdom when were mislead. He's the one who's rose up the one who bled. He's the one who keeps us optimistic, he's the reason why they created forensics. he's the one who can be jealous, that's why to him we stay constantly jealous. he's the one who they say live up above and to us all he's the one who loves.

Freeing your mind

Freeing your mind is experiencing new elements, giving you a brighter outlook on life. more favorable then what's relevant, such as marriage between a groom and his wife.
in activities that's out the ordinary, learning something new like the art of culinary.
freeing your mind,
could be you going to the max, working off an accumulated stress to help you relax. so that you can be at your best. it's giving your mind total liberty, which can help you make conscious decisions. putting you at ease filled with security, removing all the strength and tension.
Freeing your mind ,
can be listening to Sweet melodies taking you back in time clearing thoughts of infidelity as you sit down and unwind.

freeing your mind,
will be just to take a load off and doing nothing at all . A day
where you're the boss accepting no visitors and no calls.

On the other side

I heard a lot of things is different on the other side, from the
skies being blue to the beautiful tides. seeing all endangered hu-
man and creature, to being taught by that one and only teacher.
I heard the grass is greener on the other side, where you can
walk without a ride. so when the other side comes about, I'll be
there, wherever, whenever, that's without doubt.

Faithful

Within faithful you must have trust, entwined as flirtation
comes with lust. being faithful you must stay true, do unto oth-
ers as you have them do unto you. Doing what you can to walk a
straight line, just to stay faithful to your grapevine. as you walk
carefully on your toes, trying to avoid temptation and all other
foes. being faithful is strong but yet hard, when you possess it
there no limit not even the stars.

Beast

They say there's a monster in every town, just like on every sur-
face there's a clown. there's one to the west and one to the east,
its one everywhere and we call it the beast. when it comes
around it eat at your soul and spirit, just don't get close or even
come near it. He gets in your mind and make you do bad, he
can get in your thoughts and make you feel mad. Everywhere

you turn is the mark of the beast, surrounding us as if we are the meat to his feasts. when people are being evil and wicked, be the one to make the change for another ticket.

Beginning

In the beginning it was the stars, now we drive big trucks and cars. in the beginning it was just the earth, now look we have the whole universe. in the beginning it was women and men, now women dating a woman that another's plan, in the beginning it was just was a start, now we're nearly finished and it's falling apart.

Breath

To that first breath as a baby, to breathe in that first kiss from your lady. taking in oxygen from the trees, breathing in air can put you at ease. with contamination around in the air, we breathe it in rather moderate or Fair. breathing is a vital part of life, if you want your body to be right. holding it can put you on your knees, so my advice to you is better breathe.

Men and woman

Men and women are nothing alike, it's like a big and little wheel on the same bike. men are aggressive and straightforward, while women are shy and stay behind like a TV cord. men are leaders and most are brave, while women are followers and others enslaved. but women do have their up right as men let pride get them uptight. women are now much more independent while men authority is much to lenient. No matter what a person like me say, men and women are different in every way.

We see

We see everything around us, from the dirt to the big yellow school bus. we have two eyes so we can see more, from the birds in the sky to the man at the corner store. as I cover one up I still can see, I look at you, you look at me. long as we have eyes it shall forever be, to have two pair, we shall forever see.

Night and day

Different things happen between night and day, from people being civilized and going astray. a person might look like there sophisticated, but when the night comes that's when the image vacated. when its nighttime they run a smooth game, when the day comes people see what you have inside tamed. it seems like a change of character when the sunset, two people paying attention to what one people neglect. they say in this world people have two personalities, but people of the world don't realize they're actuality. when the light turns to dark real people go away don't underestimate the possibilities of the night between the day.

To be judged by man

To be judged by men was not in the plan, to be put in a box or a tin can. either in a courtroom or on the street, to be judged by man cuts the head of the sheep. to make a decision how a person look, or to judge a person calling him a crook. to judge his or her life is not in your power, You cut down your own in these las few hours. not to take heed to what I said, is unless you want to be judged by man instead.

Your will

Your will gets you up in the morning
your will is what keeps you going.

your will is your strength, your will can solve x to the 10th .
your will is what make you follow these rules, your will tells you,
you don't want to lose. your will take you to another stage
your will takes you to the next page.
your will determine what you are, your will is your power and
that's by far.

Life

I once heard "life is like a box of chocolate you never know what
you're going to get" blasting off like a rocket I'm falling deep in-
to that ditch.
life throws curves, life throws hooks, but you have to maintain.
life goes on through the book, and that's just to feed your brain.
life still move when you sit just to eat a pie, life keeps going al-
ways going even after you die.

A Rose

A rose is like life in a way, or your one true love or something
that you cherish. a rose the wind could carry it away or blossom
like a dove that petals could turn and perish.
A rose it could be like a feather, that change colors in the weath-
er. at the stem it is the backbone, of the bud which is the throne.
you pick at its petals they fall to the ground, you break a stem it
all turned around.
a rose...,

how long will it last only one person knows.

Planets

We are here on Earth and we know there is more, to Venus and
Mercury that we have yet to explore. where Mars, we have
stepped foot upon, but of all knowledge of existence there is
none. Jupiter being the biggest in shape and size. but couldn't
see it if planted with our own eyes. Saturn being the glamorous
of the most, with a ring around the outer shell forming a lumi-
nous coast. Uranus and Pluto is far too cold, about time we get
there, will be gone and of the old. everything you hear is not all
legit, until you lay eyes on all of our so-called planets.

In Conclusion,
the Comparison,
<u>to a natural Connection</u>

"The Moral"

 Emotions are everyday expression on the human anatomy. In any cause there is some type of effect, pros to cons and vice versa. Just as if it rains there then comes delays or when it's to hot plants start to wither. All in which triggers a emotion rather positive or pessimistic.

 So as we may not be able to predict or control what is so and of what our willing body offers or react to. We can adapt as individuals changing with the changing of the time. Keep in mind that it is written, " there is a season for all and for all there's a reason to everything"

 ****Utilize in what is felt towards the situations that is dealt.

 Before I leave as I have come....

The insight from a black Poet

S alutations,
     we as a people have come a long way, from old tradition, practices to laws of this present-day. results from the past has gave all people the privilege that we have now, ones being lost in a sense but now we are found. thanks be to the ancestors and to those who value a

change, putting forth the will with no limitations or durations of range.

such as Martin Luther King who had a vision within a dream, as he could grow and develop Beyond any means. even to Jeff Ward who led a supreme black liberation, to show us that we as individuals can come together as one nation. or Nat Turner who literally fought his way to be free. Ito be an example for something greater than just you and me.

we should strive to inform others on the importance of history, because without knowledge of existence its just a mere mystery. back then people used to deliberate and assemble in a fight for their rights, marching and campaigning with a voice that give off light.

those ancestors had a purpose along with a goal to reach, and when their eyes couldn't see it was for the Next generation to teach. The time now is not about the difference in our ethnic traits, but it's more on if you can afford to pay a person's financial rate.

Now there is still a thing called bias, a unquestionable separation, where you have participation, and classification, of discrimination.

some people act on certain things because of the past, while they blame and slanders others without knowing what created that mask. we as individuals don't grasp the opportunities that are made, all due to the fact of a foundation that was laid.

like now we can sit at the front of the bus and Rosa Parks did that, but when we actually get on the bus, we go straight towards the back. Sometimes we are asleep when we should be fully awake, it's because of Harriet Tubman that were led to a grand escape.

we seem to forget about the reasons for it all, and instead of knowing what we achieve we let the negativity be our downfall. Nowadays we attack each other as we destroy our own community, because of affiliation, envy, strife and of course no unity.

when it comes down to it they say May the best man win, but it's a lose-lose situation because you lost a potential brother and a friend .people usually judge the person off of what they see, but like a book if you don't open it up how do you know that is really me.

what we do as individuals reflect on the ethnic group itself ,such as involvement in sex, Fame, and how we obtain our wealth.

it's not a Mexican, Asian, black, or white thing, is about painting a broader picture with a luxurious scene. we have to move forward growing together over time. While developing in which our history should shine.

I pray there's a future where we will be able to show it, for now this is just a mere insight from a black poet.

©

Don't miss out!

Visit the website below and you can sign up to receive emails whenever Daniel Montez Barnes publishes a new book. There's no charge and no obligation.

https://books2read.com/r/B-A-VQMI-OWTZ

BOOKS 2 READ

Connecting independent readers to independent writers.

About the Author

From Atlanta, Georgia Daniel Barnes have been through many stages through the enjoyment, exploits, erratic, and essential moments. All which have been a guide and lead to a vision he shares. Coming from proverty and a life of unexpectancy. As Daniel M Barnes states and I quote " I have not triumph but have just took a step closer to victory but in time the success shall unveil prosperity, not for me but to these who need".

Read more at https://books2read.com/rl/Author-Daniel-Barnes.